Earth Striders

poems by

Kathleen McKinley Harris

Finishing Line Press
Georgetown, Kentucky

Earth Striders

For Eloise Haight McKinley who read poetry—and anything else I wanted—to me during my childhood. She read by the hour until she was hoarse when I was young and often very sick. She argued the case for owning horses for her girls.

This, too, is for my daughters, Susannah and Elizabeth, and for Everett.

Copyright © 2017 by Kathleen McKinley Harris
ISBN 978-1-63534-349-6 First Edition
All rights reserved under International and Pan-American Copyright Conventions. No part of this book may be reproduced in any manner whatsoever without written permission from the publisher, except in the case of brief quotations embodied in critical articles and reviews.

ACKNOWLEDGMENTS

Grateful acknowledgment to the publications in which some of these poems first appeared, sometimes in slightly different words:

Blueline, "Pearl" and "Work Ethic"
Ilsley Library Publication, "The Road to Eden"
Otter Creek Poets: By the Waterfall, "The Lesson"
Vermont Life, "Bear Fear"
Willard & Main VIII, "Haying"
Willard & Main XI, "Riding Horseback"

Thanks to my friend, Nancy Means Wright, for her encouragement to me ever since she read a short story of mine in a workshop she was teaching through the League of Vermont Writers. Thanks also to Frances O'Reilly, horsewoman, and Prof. John Clagett who approved of my poems. Thanks also to Susan Bartlett Weber, and to David Weinstock who had a wonderful idea 19 years ago for a weekly meeting of a group, the Otter Creek Poets. And to Margery G. Sharp, my partner in a newspaper publishing adventure, and also to friends, Barbara and Howard Seaver, Dale Hyerstay, Polly Heininger, Bob Essman, and Barbara Scribner.

Publisher: Leah Maines

Editor: Christen Kincaid

Cover Art: Douglas Scribner

Author Photo: Barbara Seaver

Cover Design: Elizabeth Maines McCleavy

Printed in the USA on acid-free paper.
Order online: www.finishinglinepress.com
also available on amazon.com

Author inquiries and mail orders:
Finishing Line Press
P. O. Box 1626
Georgetown, Kentucky 40324
U. S. A.

Table of Contents

Bear Fear 1

Sunny Girl 3

Winter Afternoon 5

The Logger 7

Horse Trading 9

Buggy Trips 10

The Roof Goes 12

Pearl 13

Haying 15

Making a Living 17

Work Ethic 18

Building 20

The Road to Eden 22

Riding Horseback 24

High Mowing 25

So Why Were We Allowed to Ride? 26

Fence Posts 27

The Pooka 28

The Lesson 30

August at Dusk 32

"Think, when we talk of horses, that you see them."
                                        Henry the Fifth

BEAR FEAR

While we were growing up,
with the land reverting to woods around us
and over the ridge of McKinstry Hill
the wildness of the Diggins
and ours the last house on two dusty tracks
with grass in the middle brushing the oil pan,
we sat around the woodstove before bedtime
when company came and the men told tales
of boundary disputes, ghosts, and bears,
but we didn't believe the one-handed World War II veteran,
the land surveyor, who said, *I never carry a weapon.*
There is not an animal in the Vermont woods
which is not afraid of me—except for man.
We children, brought up on bear
stories, grew fearful to walk old sugar woods roads.
We sang and whistled and shouted
to fend off bobcats and bears and our racket
worked until one October when we went to pick
apples from a gnarled tree shading the cellar hole
on Old Wilson Road. A terrible stench—everyone said
bears smelled awful—and then we saw dribbles
and piles of steaming chewed up apple vomit.
The bear had gorged to spilling over.
Heavy with winter fat and wanting more,
he had climbed the apple tree, broken a trunk,
snapped off limbs, strewn leaves on the ground.
We backed away and ran.
We knew, too, how once our cousin went for the cows at dawn,
and from behind a steeple bush, a she bear reared up.
He stood between her and her cubs.
He shot her and both cubs with three lucky shots.
Later, he found he had only those three bullets.
We heard gossip about the neighbor boy
the other boys teased about not hunting.

The fall finally he went deer hunting, a bear
chased him across an open field
and he thought he was a goner for sure
until he came to a summer camp, dove headfirst
through a window. A search party found him.
We saw the little pane he shattered and wondered
how ever did a boy his size squeeze through?
We knew most horses spook at bears.
But the previous owner said
he had seen bears in their pasture
when our horses were his, so we did not fret
about bears that sunset when we steered
our horses up the steep road toward the Diggins.
While the horses were blowing, catching their breath
after their climb, and we talked, a black animal surprisingly
no bigger than a dog nor more significant hustled
across the road and into the golden rod.
The horses, glad for flat going after the grade,
did not bolt or shy, and my glimpse of the long-feared one
was so brief, afterwards, I never
was sure I hadn't made up a bear
that night we rode into the Diggins.

SUNNY GIRL

When first I saw our neighbor, Vern,
he was riding astride his flashy, registered,
Tennessee Walker stallion, Better Chance.
I was eleven when on his carefully groomed,
snorting, prancing stallion, he and his horse
passed by our house each afternoon.

When first I saw Sunny Girl, his new mare,
a Tennessee Walker, Vern had sold his stallion.
For years he'd tried to buy that 14-year-old.
I took in his new Tennessee Walker
mare as he rode past our house.
I knew he'd found his dream horse.

When first I saw the strawberry roan mare,
my brain filled up with horses, and I started to
hang out at Vern's barn with the barn girl gang.
I knew there never lived a finer horse than Sunny Girl
and learned a new jargon—like gait, running walk,
and: strawberry roan is chestnut with white hairs.

When first I saw Sunny Girl, I read up on her breed,
learned how plantation owners with lots of land, bred
her breed with gaits easy to ride hours over many acres.
Where Vern's stallion was volatile, unpredictable, scary,
she, though big at 16.2 hands high,
was kindness, gentleness—and spirit.

When first I saw her, as if she were food, I had to own her.
Instead, I settled for a pinto Vern found in a back pasture,
bargain steed my sister and I could afford with our savings.
The eight-year-old pinto mare we bought balked at taking
a step, lame as she was from grown-out, untrimmed hooves
and grossly overweight from too much green spring grass.

When first we tried out our fat pinto, we had blind trust
in Vern's horse savvy— and faith maybe some distant day
we'd think he'd struck a good deal for us.
When we sisters rode, our pact was we'd ride our mare
turn-about every other day. But often, on my off day,
kind Vern let me tack up Sunny Girl, so both of us rode.

When first I groomed Sunny Girl, I found
her stable manners quiet and calm
with no nasty surprises, but more astonishing,
when first I rode the Tennessee Walker mare
was her long-strided walk and instant response
to the slightest flick of my heels on her flanks,

when at my asking, as if she guessed my wish, she glided
into her running walk and it was like riding water flow,
an effortless gait easy to sit for a day-long ride. Then
I gathered her reins to ask for the canter from a walk, and
she transitioned into her rocking horse gait— I asked why
a rider would choose to trade a mare like this for a trotter?

When first I wished, true lover that I was, to own Sunny Girl,
the barn talk was old Mrs. B. whose barn had quarters where
an Irishman lived in exchange for caring for her horses—
Mrs. B. decided if she owned Sunny Girl, she'd ride pain-free.
She told Vern to name his price—but he wouldn't deal.
Sunny Girl was aged when he bought her. Yet,

when first he had her in his barn, he decided
to have her bred. But she was old
and it didn't take and didn't take.
Years later when at last she was with foal
and gave him a colt, as if he were the father,
he sent out birth announcements.

WINTER AFTERNOON

Vern insisted each horse in his barn drive.
Snowy winter days, he hitched a horse in turn
to a homemade sled, a cart he'd rigged on old skis,
not runners, the better to make use
of the least snow cover. So each horse
every fifth day was exercised in dead of winter.
I, and every horse-crazy neighborhood kid,
could recite every fact about every horse
Vern owned: height in hands, weight, breeding,
age, good and bad habits.
We children of the neighborhood
heard our Pied Piper's sleigh bells
ringing in the biting winter wind,
long before we spotted horse, sled, driver.
Anxious to catch him, we dressed,
booted up, ran out, hoped the old horseman
would have room for all—and just maybe
this afternoon he'd invite us to climb aboard.
Generous, he usually did.
The horse of the day snorted white puffs
from its nostrils, pranced before we offered correctly
on the flat of a hand, an apple. With white,
fragrant juice slobber foaming from its mouth,
since the bit made it hard to chew the treat, the horse
was occupied with apple taste while we scrambled on.
Then Vern, a large presence in bulky wools, clucked
to the horse, slapped the leather reins on its rump,
and we trotted off. Always I felt pride and superior
to be aboard, the same way a person on horseback
feels toward a man on foot. Then, to watch
the action in the hindquarters, legs, swishing tail,
feel the rhythm of the walk or trot, listen
to the music of brass and bronze bells
jingle-jangling, see the fuzzy winter hair
on horse flanks with dark lines of sweat forming,

white snowballs building up under horse feet,
flecks of white foam flying, hear hooves beat
the hard road, the sliding scrape of ski runners,
sense the power of the horse pulling smartly,
the pent-up excitement of the spirited animal,
observe the cold turning all our cheeks apple-red.
I wanted to ask Vern to teach me to drive,
and I, a child, never, ever, dared.

THE LOGGER

Warn't my land to start, but by and by,
got my hands on the deed. Knowed better than my cousin
what to do with the home place. Yes, sir. Sold the farm—
half the farm to be 100 percent accurate—after I logged off.
Took every goddamn stick of timber worth a cent.
Took the city feller, too. Ha! Sold him the no-good house—
not a true line in it. Last folks rented it off of me—
shiftless—regular hillbillies. With a woods full
of kindling growing around, come winter, they ripped
off the wainscoting from the summer kitchen.
Burned it for firewood. Skipped out in the night
on the rent, too. Left their last supper on the table to rot.
Ought to set a match to the house.
Drafty old cow barn, 'bout to fall in—worthless—
and sixty straight up-and-down acres.
I kept t'other sixty of standing timber.
Course, when the city feller saw the property,
there was a milk house and a dandy horse barn, too.
I knowed it was the wife's doing. Was she as which wanted it.
Thought she'd faint dead away first time
she saw the view open up before her. I watched
her almost fall back against the mister.
"It's the most beautiful place I've ever seen," says she.
She spoke the truth there: you can see all the way
from Elmore Mountain clear to Belvidere.
A woman like that lives for beauty.
You bet I piped up. *Million dollar view.*
Ticked off the property's good points.
*Best tasting water in the whole state of Vermont—
a never-fail spring.* Didn't hear
nothing from the feller till winter.
He sent me a letter and a good bank check
just before mud season. Came out of that deal
smelling like a rose. Going to Florida next mud season.

While it was still froze up solid, took my winch
and this here rig and drug the horse barn on logs
two miles down to Centerville. Set it on a new foundation.
Made me the best house I ever lived in.
Heard tell the mister sputtered some come summer
when he found the only square building on the place
had walked off and nothing but field stones to show
where the horse barn stood. Ha! Nothing in the way
of the wife's view now. Been logging those sixty I kept
up on Jane Ann Hill. Folks below want to stay out of my way
when I head down with my truck and a full load of fresh-cut logs.
No brakes. You bet it's safe. You can hear the gears grind
half a mile away. A dead man could hear me coming.
I'm a-goin' at a pretty good clip time I hit Morrisville.
Four miles downhill, all the way.
Now, I got to make me a dooryard stop at the farm
as which the city feller owns now—fill these water jugs.
Your father t'home, girl? What say
you run get him while I climb down?
(Knew he'd come a-running when he saw 'twas me.)
Young feller, something I've been needing to speak to you about.
When you locked up and went home to where you come from,
you unhitched the pipe to the horse trough.
Now, I can't let you get away with that. Folks always stop
at the trough to water their horses or add to their radiators.
Always have. Always will. After you packed up,
I had to climb up the hill and fix it back the way it's always been.
Way it's supposed t'be. Now watch them girls of yours good
when I drive by with a load of spruce or hemlock or
 balsam like these monster logs, you hear?
No brakes on this here rig of mine.

HORSE TRADING

Albert told Burnie
who told Carl
Gypsy Dougal sold
to Ed's father
Floyd's fancy bay mare—
the steed George wanted.
Homer watched the affair,
and so did Ivory Junior
as they devoured fried dough
during the hour the boys rested
in Jack's rig hitched in Ken's hayfield,
the buggy Lon leased for the
annual agricultural fair
at Morristown Corners.
Norton noticed coin change hands.
Oliver, too, observed the switcheroo.
Perley perceived Ed's dad set a smart pace
away with Floyd's fancy bay
harnessed to his buggy traces
from the Morristown Corners Fair.
*Gypsy Dougal bartered Ed's crow-bait
for Floyd's fancy bay?* queried Quentin.
Righto, Robert remarked.
Ed's family worked the bay beauty
through her prime and in time
retired her to clover on Sam's back forty.
In the Post Office sixty years following
the bargain, said Tom to Urban:
A good horse ten times over.
What'd the town do? asked Vern.
Old Sheriff Wade allowed,
*I figured as how 'twas their own gol-durn
affair.* Xerses, Yancey, and Zeke opted
against investigation, also.
Yammering zestily about yesteryear
and the Yankee-gypsy horse swap
four old codgers exited the PO.

BUGGY TRIPS

This is the high hill farm Mother and Dad bought
with a raspberry patch, brook full of trout,
an open-armed apple tree for climbing,
a spring-fed watering trough with frogs,
a green pasture where the neighbor's cows graze,
and a grey barn shaky on its foundation.

This is Daddy and Grandpa exploring the barn
with its loft, cow stanchions, manure pit, cobwebs,
light and shadow I dream of playing in.

This is Daddy and Grandpa forbidding
the barn to me and my little sister. Then they
discover a two-wheeled carriage in the barn.
They shout, lift us sisters onto the buggy seat.

This is Daddy and Grandpa seizing the shafts,
hauling the buggy clattering on ironclad wheels
over dirt road from barn onto lawn.

This is the buggy's last road trip to its
resting place near the raspberry patch.
This is the beginning of imaginary trips
for me, for Jane, and cousin Victor.

This is the whip holder, so one of us
must cut a willow switch of just
the right thickness to fit and swish it
through the air to make a lazy horse trot.

We girls must beg cookies from Mother
to wrap in a burdock leaf for lunch.
One of us raises the leather cushion.
Cleverly hidden beneath is a hinged lid.
Poke two fingers through round holes.
Lift. Pack lunch in secret compartment.

In turn Jane, Victor, and I each place
a foot on the iron step-up. The buggy
seat has room for all three of us.
We're off! Sometimes Victor drives.

Sometimes Jane or I handle the reins.
We drive to Morrisville for groceries
or to Burlington for the dentist or
to Lake Eden for a swim or even
stay overnight in Niagara Falls or
travel to London to visit the Queen.

Sometimes the horse misbehaves—
and then how we bounce on the seat
and the buggy springs tip up and down.
We talk about the day we'll buy a horse,
  keep him in the barn and really drive to town.

THE ROOF GOES

This is the summer the barn roof goes.
Few hand-hewn beams remain in place.
Then the barn falls down, and through
buggy wheel spokes grass grows hay-high.
The buggy wood weathers gray.
Its punky floorboards crack and break.
Iron step and whip holder rust. Horsehair
stuffing bursts through upholstery.

This is Grandpa gathering paper, kindling,
slab pine. *What are you doing, Grandpa?*
It's time to burn it.
Not our buggy, Grandpa!
It's dangerous for you children.
Please, not our buggy!

But he is grown-up. Grandpa has decided.
His fire crackles in the pine pitch,
makes a show. Flames lick along gray wood
buggy frame, seat, flare the length of its
long shafts. We three and Grandpa
watch the pyre until only iron trim,
springs, step, wheel rims, whip holder,
charred grass, and ashes litter the ground.
No more trips. Nothing left for a real horse
to pull. I cry and cry, knowing I'm growing
out of child world—what is the world
I'm growing into?

PEARL

We waited until late in June when there came an afternoon
finally when the neighbors' big girls were free to play,
after the steel hay fork fell then hoisted the last bite,
a third of a wagon load of loose hay and insects into the steaming loft
and the daughters had no more mown and tedded grass to rake
into cocks nor stubble to slash bloody their bare feet
as they sweated side-by-side in the field's scented heat
with their daddy, brother, and the team.
There were five of us girls counting their three
and Pearl was oldest and our leader that afternoon
when we hiked the high hill pasture above their house
and she showed us a porcupine den and higher
where a brook flowed into a grassy bubble of a pool.
Then Pearl leaped onto the gray stone wall to lead
us all running lightly like tightrope walkers
on the grid of the farm's stone walls,
and breathlessly following Pearl, we ran
to the line fence and everybody's favorite climbing tree,
a sugar maple, its wide, welcoming arms
an easy reach even for little Rosalie.
I prided myself on my tree-climbing prowess,
on how much farther I could climb than other girls
because I took pains to test each branch carefully.
But Pearl ascended so high my neck hurt from looking up
before she came down and dropped to the ground
and chose next the first tree in the fence row,
a wild cherry I judged too young to be a climbing tree. Thin, sinewy
Pearl used the cherry limbs and those of a nearby slender sapling
as ladder's rungs until I could see only sky among glistening green leaves,
and a flash of her white legs and her tan toes gripping the tree's red bark.
Watch this! sang out Pearl as arm over arm, like an arboreal ancestor,
she swung from cherry to sapling to another and another tree
above the lichen-covered feldspar and quartzite boulders
while I tried not to picture her flesh and dark hair
broken and spilled over the rocks if her hand slipped by chance
or if she grabbed a dead branch, guessing it would hold

her slight weight and it didn't, until she, queen
of tree-climbers, joined us safe in the maple's dappled light.
Next summer, Pearl, champion girl-climber, wore shoes and dresses,
and Pearl, who always ran, walked arm-in-arm with a man.

HAYING

In the still air of a scorcher of a June morning
steady, repetitive sounds start in the hayfield
on our neighbor's side of the stonewall.
Back when days passed on our dirt road
without a car going by, small sounds
of cutting bar, harness, and whiffletree chains
carried just as morning and evening our neighbor
calling his cows, *Come, Boss. Come, Boss* floated
on the air. From lookouts high in our apple tree's limbs
Jane and I see our friends' Daddy cutting his hay.

Round and round the rawboned gray workhorse treads,
cutter bar laying flat the long grass while field birds fly up,
frantic about horse's hooves, large as dinner plates,
ironshod, stomping nearer and nearer their eggs and hatchlings.
Then silence until after lunch when again voices
call from the field, unsettle its stillness.

Round and round Steve is driving the bay
in smaller and smaller circles, raking
the yellowing, drying hay into windrows.
Lured, we run down the road into the hayfield.
Laurabelle and Pearl, with broad-brimmed bonnets
shading their necks and shoulders, grip
tall wooden rakes whose teeth are pegs.
They're raking scatterings into hay tumbles.

Only Rosalie, too small to hay, waves,
jumps up and down when she sees Jane and me.
The air is moist, saturated with scent of curing hay.

The new-mown field looks soft as green moss.
Our friends are barefoot, so we follow their lead,
leave our shoes at field's edge, run a few steps toward Rosalie
until my un-callused, embarrassingly bone-white foot
lands with the heft of my body's weight on stubble

stick-thick and drill-sharp which stabs my flesh,
draws blood-beads. Defeated, I blink away pain, hope to pick
a route back to my shoes with no more puncture wounds.

Round and round Steve drives the dump-rake, his face
and work-hard, bare arms sun-baked bronze as the bay horse.
I guess why he turns out for a mound of gray stones.
But why rake crooked circles and leave standing
around some stakes, high manes of grass?
Laurabelle and Pearl can't quit raking to explain,
so Rosalie says, *Birds' nests. We hope we find them all.*
We're children. We, not having work to do, tire of heat,
tire of watching work which doesn't change. We run off
to play, not knowing on that June day soon all foreverlastingly
for always will change. Knowing, I'd have watched—
and taken notes.

MAKING A LIVING

The land in the lower pasture remembered:
three or four long plowed furrows were proof
the last farmer gave up before he finished plowing,
before he harrowed and planted a crop. Where last
he broke the sod, the turned up earth stayed put.
Once, I led an expedition of girls to a mammoth stone pile.
We passed the grassy, rolling lines of that last plowing
and found the pile nothing except hot, boring stones.
Of sweat and hard labor we didn't know enough to dwell
on the hands that picked that heap of stone.
The exploring child learns every secret in a house or property.
Near the stone pile in a sunny hollow, I found stretched out,
ligaments relaxed as if asleep, a white horse skeleton complete,
I judged, in every bone, a marvel of Tinker Toy parts.
Hay-tall grasses and Queen Anne's lace grew twined
among its ribs, vertebrae, and legs. Teeth intact in its jaw,
the giant head seemed long as I was. An archaeological prize
in the pasture, its hundred bones, my private treasure—
and now the grown-ups must stop and come, be awe-filled.
Next, I must carry my trophy head to my room.
But Grandfather said, *You must not touch it.*
It might harbor disease. How could this clean,
sun-bleached white thing, rain and snow-washed,
cause sickness? Not hold my lifetime find in my hands?
I have a pair of longhorn cattle horns I'll give you
for your bones. My horse disappeared—the cattle horns
were worthless compared to my horse skeleton.
In the years since I was ten, I've put the clues together:
The renter who burned up the summer kitchen wainscoting
plowed those furrows with that horse in his last farming try.
He pushed the old or sick animal beyond its strength
to plant a crop, maybe a cash crop, maybe hops,
for Grandfather identified volunteers nearby.
After a few furrows, the horse died in his harness.
The farmer, undone by his grim run of luck,
abandoned the carcass to scavengers.

WORK ETHIC

It's different, our father explained.
*This summer you must pay for candy
and soda pop you take from behind the counter.
Your great aunt and uncle have been too good.* They've
allowed too many in town to run up big tabs,
and they're too kind to ask poor people to pay up.
That summer Great Uncle kept half a dozen young Jerseys
in his mother's small barn down the road where
there was no pasture, so he cut fresh green hay with a scythe
as feed, milked morning and night before he opened the store.

Next summer Great Aunt and Uncle's general store and garage
with its red flying horse sign and a complete house upstairs
—back verandah, kitchen, dining room,
living room, long hall, bedrooms—had new owners.
And Great Aunt and Uncle owned a large, rundown farm
across the valley on Battle Row. Great Uncle, his sons, and hired men
replaced every ruined fence on the place with sound, stout cedar posts
and three taut wires, cleared fencerows, first time in fifty years.
Even I, a child, could see the pastures and fields come back,
hear pride in Great Uncle's voice at what he'd done with vision, hard work,
and will—a new beginning when he and Great Aunt were not young,
he whose recreation was going to Hicks' weekly cattle auction—
success depending not solely on the land
but also on his being a fine judge of cows—
or driving on the Bayley-Hazen Road on a cool evening.
My father worried Great Aunt didn't have enough fun in her life.

Great Uncle couldn't understand how my father could let
his land grow up into weed trees, blackberries, ferns—
not keep the fields and pastures clean.
Great Uncle's standards inside his barn were as high
as outside. Children were not allowed to jump
in his hay mow and damage the cows' feed.
His gutters were cleaned immediately, strewn with bedding.
He received a premium for his milk's low bacterial count.

My father pointed out Great Aunt's cleanliness in the milk house
contributed to their achievement, gave credit where it was due.
We'd talk about horses, Great Uncle and I.
I'd tell him about my mare. He told me how he hated
to trade his horses for a dirty, smelly, noisy tractor.
Then the times forced him to give up his beautiful Jerseys
for Holsteins, put in a bulk tank, too.

I thought I'd buy goats to clear my parents' land,
they being cheap enough for a child to afford.
He took my idea seriously, told me in detail why I must not
 turn to goats—too troublesome—to eat invasive plants.
Daily Great Aunt fried doughnuts for his breakfast.
He lived on fresh doughnuts, pie, coffee, cigarettes,
meat and potatoes, doomed himself to stomach cancer—
finally died of it. He milked the day he died.

BUILDING

You came first to the hill farm
to supervise your FFA boys hired
to rotary-mow the lower pasture
for my parents. You stayed for dinner.

I, on impulse deciding to buy a horse,
when my young brother blurted out he
wanted to ride, too, without careful
consideration, I bought two young mares
and hired my brother and his friend

to help me fence the 10-acre pasture
with its open, year-round, flowing brook.
When the truck delivered the mares, I
turned them loose—an impractical purchase,
for only the three-year-old could be ridden—

the unschooled two-year-old, not for a new rider.
In Vermont winter is inevitable,
and where the old barn once presided,
now grew head-tall, rich grass flourishing
on the remains of the manure pit. Without fail,

my mares must have shelter. Together
you and I began to plan a pole shed:
we'd site it among the grafted apple trees.
All the time I thought we were just friends—
I never guessed you were strategizing.

You said a proper foundation wasn't needed.
You knew exactly what to purchase. So
I bought green, rough-sawn spruce lumber
from a North Hyde Park mill. In addition,
the mill owner volunteered I could have

for free all the sawdust I wanted for bedding.
With your skills and strength the shed rose fast,
the boards fragrant of deep woods. What fun
for the two of us, young, working together:
magically the shed went up. You solved the roof

problem I hadn't thought about when you offered
me old barn roof tin you'd saved. There was rust
and holes, but we patched and caulked.
My mares had shelter before snowfall,
and you, you became a regular dinner guest.

THE ROAD TO EDEN

That early spring when trees were yet bare
before sunset in the slanted gold of afternoon,
I ride my three-year-old mare.

Each evening as her endurance, power,
and muscle built after an idle winter,
I extended our ride until it stretched an hour.

We trot past Fitzgeralds, Browns, Old Scott's,
canter by beaver pond, cellar holes with century-large lilacs,
spring-visible lots unknown dead folks fenced with grey rocks,

by apple trees, their unpruned limbs suffocating, black with rot,
where young conifers spread through an orchard remnant.
Where the road narrows, my mare slows to a trot

as if she understands we have ventured into darkness
far enough. Only a woods path, once road,
waits where night like a wall lies before us.

I turn my mare toward home, light, and open fields,
her young horse skittishness worked out,
both of us easy. She, now content to walk, yields.

Her neck, wet with hot sweat, glistens.
Her breath forms white cloud puffs in the cold air.
I relax my hands and legs, observe and listen.

For birdsong, in the season it is too early,
but snowmelt flows from shadowed drifts,
gurgles about tree roots, swells ditches, runs hurly-burly.

On our road—suddenly a penisula of high-banked gravel ledge—
run-off water has almost stranded my mare and me
when I spot on a hummock not yet hidden in leafy foliage,

among the popples and willows in swollen bud
a white marble marker I've never noticed before,
raised up on a mound, above the flood.

Requesting the halt, I squeeze the reins.
While I read the epitaph and date,
my young mare dances, eager for her grain.

*Lafayette Hyde Shot Himself Accidentally Here
Aged 16 Years 17 Days 1857.*
I ride my mare home, chilled with night fear.

Later, I had his story from an old man, a neighbor.
*The boy got liquored up one night—
went to the widow's house and raped her.*

*It's the first cellar hole down the road on the right—
the one with big lilacs. Next morning,
sober, he shot himself in broad daylight.*

So the boy, with a hero's name, never reached twenty— lost.
They buried his spilled, young blood in a grave,
not in the churchyard but where the roads crossed.

RIDING HORSEBACK

Riding horseback, climbing a washboard dirt road up,
up to the saddle of the hills where the view
of farms and Sterling range reaches far as the Adirondacks,
past two ponds, past the farm with fallen-in
house and barn last farmed in the 1940s,
past barbed wire fence strands and rotting posts,
past the neighbor's now un-grazed heifer pasture
where a bear killed one of the young cows last summer,
past where once we saw a bear cub at sunset,
our horses breathing hard over the height
and then the relief of the downhill road,
soon petering out to trail into the valley of the Diggins
and riding horseback, splashing through the deep mud hole
where motored vehicles decide to turn around,
riding, riding past a tarpaper hunting camp
near clatter of a swollen, rushing brook
out of the woods over land once farm fields
until finding a ford, kicking the horses across
and they grunt, dig in, carry us out of the rank, green
grasses, alders, and flowing water of the streambed
to a bank top and the side of a town-maintained gravel road—
and no time to voice or point to what we both saw
stretched full-length along a horizontal branch
barn beam thick of an at least two hundred year old maple,
among junk tree growth, green leaves, sunlight
and mottled shadows almost concealing
the big, blocky head facing us, tufted ears,
oversized glowing eyes of a nocturnal animal,
a cat's body, and before we could speak,
but not before fear hit of how my mare would react
if the big cat sprang onto her sweaty rump,
soundlessly it faded, melded into the foliage,
part again of the light and shadow—
and our eyes not keen enough to follow.

HIGH MOWING

Some sun-filled, air-still, blue-sky August noon climb up
among headed-out timothy, redtop, and orchard grass
where popple seedlings, goldenrod, ferns, steeple bush,
black-eyed Susans, and wild strawberries stake claim
to a high mowing–land last horse-harvested for gain.

Climb up and sit down on the warm earth.
Grasses rise high to form a screen filtering
out the gasp-grab-camera mountain view.
For this half hour let sun, sky, air, earth, grass,
rounds and sounds of insects and birds be the measure.

For this moment, register sickness and terror,
poverty and injustice, politics and money,
weddings and deaths below the horizon,
beyond the field of vision. Crickets sing
a sustained treble. Locusts buzz as if

they're some yet to be named bird species.
Glistening dragonflies or damselflies glide by—
for this moment, names don't matter—
their paper-crisp rainbow wings click, clatter.
At intervals, flies drone; bees light on blossoms, hum.

In the fencerow among glittering, gossiping popples,
robins chirp warning. Jays scream. Chickadees call.
Heedless to threats, insects feed. Untouched by whatever
predator prowls in the next field, goldfinches sing.
Breathe in and out this blue-sky half hour on a high mowing.

SO WHY WERE WE ALLOWED TO RIDE?

About great granddad, Archibald MacLean—
of his passion for horses, this concerning
a certain light carriage horse— but about Archie,
let me say how he culled out and saved all the little potatoes.
Then during interminable Vermont winters each morning
he cooked them up in a big pot on the back of the kitchen woodstove
so his horses would have a warm breakfast—and also
before breakfast he built the rest of the fires in the household:
in the kitchen cook-stove,
in the back parlor,
in Allie's room,
in the barn trough
because his darling horses needed warm water—
and then, too, cows give more milk with warm water to drink.
Dad said his granddad was the most generous man he ever knew—
why, once, he in a river run saved half a dozen men who fell off
behemoth logs into roiling water, although some swear maybe he saved
even a bigger number of drowning men, such a strong swimmer he was.
But about his buying of this horse—in light of the friendship
between two Scotsmen, during the summer I was twelve, my father
paid a call on Bruce MacDonald who in his prime was the blacksmith.
Bruce sat in dusky shadow in his dim-lit antique shop
full of dank, cast-off furniture, dust kitties, clutter round about.
I told him times over not to buy him. 'Archie, mon, for sure, he's a killer.'
But Archie would have it: 'Whist, Bruce, with kindness, any horse
can be gentled.' Last thing before bed, the old horseman always
checked on the horses— only this once, he did not speak
to the carriage horse before entering the stall.
The horse kicked him and with his hooves, struck him
in the chest, kicked him in the stall, trampled him.
His son-in-law pulled him out, and the horse broke both
the younger man's legs as he dragged the old man out.
They phoned Archie's daughter in Canada to come to her dad.
Do you see the beautiful light? he asked her, a few mornings later.
Yes, his daughter told him, to give him comfort: *I see the light—*
although she didn't. Then, he died. After, for the remainder of his life,
my grandfather walked with canes— so why were we allowed to ride?

FENCE POSTS

We need pasture for the newly purchased
pony and, yes, the widow lady, Ella, will rent
her unused land to us, a two-minute walk
for our 12 and eight-year-old girls, this will work.
We parents saw owning horses means
the children will learn what it takes to care
for a fragile, dependent creature. If our girls
were to own horses, they would feed,
water, exercise, walk, call the vet, farrier,
and seller of fence posts, do it all.
Ella's land with a view, cleared in the 1790s,
was unfenced. A classified advertised
fence posts in Jeffersonville. Yes,
we could pick them up that evening. First,
a math problem: the girls and their father
had to figure how many fence posts
would do the job. Then we four rode
in Everett's Ford Ranger to pick them up
in the golden spring evening with the haze
of all things possible surrounding
our newly purchased, yet unknown pony.
We reached the fence post place.
A young couple had given up dairying,
their huge, ark of a barn now over-large storage
for a used furniture venture. Fresh-cut and unpeeled
posts filled the air with the pungent, practically
overpowering woods scent of green lumber
before we saw the giant pile of cedar fence posts.
The girls and their father loaded 75 rock-heavy posts
into the truck body which is most of what
the younger daughter remembers of the night.
But then in the golden early spring evening, birds
began to circle as they hunted insects
and called *Whip-Poor-Will, Whip-Poor-Will*—
the only time I've ever heard Whip-Poor-Wills
in Vermont. Their calls mingled with run-off gurgles
from vegetation so flattened from snow blanket
weight I question how grass ever will grow again.
This is my memory of the night we bought fence posts.

THE POOKA

> *The Pooka seems essentially an animal spirit. Some derive his name from poc, a he-goat; and speculative persons consider him the forefather of Shakespeare's "Puck."*
> — William Butler Yeats

Shape-changing spirit:
sometime horse, goat, goblin,
I should have been forewarned.

He was a blooded, "flea-bitten-gray" Connemara
with generations of dams and sires listed on his papers.
If you didn't know horse colors, you'd call him white.

Oh, I should have been wary when we tried him out
in early spring on a mud season day
before the green growth surge began.

I had no foreshadowing as I was leading him when
without warning he bucked at the end of the lead-line.
After, the seller asked, *Do you still want to buy him?*

But he was such a beauty—and he was registered. And
they say the breed possesses dense bones from generations
of Connemaras raised on lush, limestone Irish pastures.

Why, Connemara hooves are so hard, he'll never need shoes,
only occasional trimming by a farrier. Beguiled by his beauty,
I choose not to comprehend what the owner's question meant.

So I bought the gelding, Pooka, and took him home.
Our girls shared him, the first pony we owned,
meaning there was no time for me to ride him

until at last one day there came an afternoon
during the getting-to-know-him-spell
when it worked for me to take him out.

He had no problem going alone.
He was not a barn rat.
I rode him a mile by the side of the road.

I turned around, and all was well.
His walk was smooth. It was balmy.
What could be more pleasant

than a ride on a good horse in spring? But
I was doing exactly what a rider must never do:
I was not concentrating on the ride.

A trustworthy, good horse
will take care of the rider. But
this Connemara was Pooka,

named for a spirit, elfin character,
a shape-changer. Be careful
what you name things, for

a name can be a prediction.
No sooner did I yield to soft, spring air,
gurgling water sound, and the joy of the ride,

no sooner did I let my attention wander,
than Pooka, the trickster, sensed my lack
of concentration. From a sedate walk

he twisted into a rodeo-worthy buck,
impossible to sit. I landed at his feet.
My right elbow struck the pavement hard.

Pain radiated into my shoulder. Dazed, I scrambled
upright, reins tight in my hand. Got back on. And woefully,
woefully rode home. The Pooka had taught a lesson.

THE LESSON

We are captivated as the 14-year-old
stands at her pony's head. She checks
whether we, her family, watch
through frost-etched windows while
Pooka's breath clouds in frozen air,
stubs of icicles already forming
on his muzzle and eyelashes
before she plays out the lunge line
through her fingers. She orders,
Walk, and he obeys, a white pony
working for a girl in a field of white,
against the pink sky of a winter afternoon.
As girls and women always read
their beauty from others' eyes,
my daughter judges the pair of them:
she, pre-woman; her pony, Pooka,
snow-showered immaculately white,
his long, wavy mane and tail
and her long, honey ponytail
flying, a picture full of grace we could
not turn away from as she pivots,
black lunge whip elevated in her black gloved hand.
We applaud her mastery of the difficult pony
as he circles around her, magically
held in place at walk, trot, halt
by a thin line and her confidence.
Before she asks him for the canter,
he tosses his head. Through my window
I observe a twisted look in his eyes—
he is too pony-wily to submit willingly—
his nostrils flare red, tail swishes. He
tears the lunge line loose from her hand, plunges,
bucks, explodes across the unblemished snow,
lunge line trailing behind like a blood red streamer.
She'll be hurt! Grandmother wails
as the white pony snorts, digs in his heels.

He sprints back and forth, so much horsepower
galloping across the white landscape
while Grandmother wrings her hands,
cries her chorus from window to window,
She'll be hurt! Do something.

The girl is a point of quiet.
My impulse is to rush out, fix things, protect.
But I say, *She knows what she is doing.*
She has the skill. And Grandfather,
my dad, stands beside me. *Do not*
be afraid to let them live their lives.
Eventually, the pony tires,
stops short, like a western horse,
with a shake of his head and mane.
My daughter smiles at our window,
lights up winter's deepening dark.
She strides toward her white pony.

AUGUST AT DUSK

The sun has dropped below Sterling Mountain.
freeing for the brief night hours the pasture
of endless summer sun's incessant beating heat.
In relief the grasses breathe out vapors.

In the rising, warm air stream,
like a kind thought before a friend speaks,
we sense in the night a benign presence
before their huge, dark bodies take shape.

Our two mares, expecting gentle hands,
after generations of their kind and ours sharing lives—
interrupt their serious night grazing to greet us.
They breathe on us as we stroke their softness—
their breath, ours, the earth's intermingling.

Kathleen McKinley Harris is a graduate of Middlebury College and has a master's in English from Case Western Reserve University. She has attended the Breadloaf Writers' Conference and the Vermont Studio Center. William Morrow, Jr. published her children's book, *The Wonderful Hay Tumble*, in 1988. Her poem, "Bear Fear," won the 1999 Ralph Nading Hill, Jr. Literary Award. Her poems have been published in *Vermont Ink, Snowy Egret, Potato Eyes, Willard & Maple VIII, The Society of Children's Book Writers and Illustrators' Bulletin, Vermont Life, Blueline, Avocet*; she is the 1999 third place winner in *The Comstock Review* poetry contest and was a finalist in the 2001 *Sow's Ear Poetry Review's Contest*. Her poem, "Cat from the Animal Shelter," appeared in June Cotner's anthology, *Animal Blessings* (Harper, 2000). She also writes historical articles. She is a former teacher (kindergarten at Pierpont, Ohio; high school at Morrisville and Hyde Park, Vt; fiction and poetry at the University of Illinois, Urbana) and for several years co-published and edited an every-other-week newspaper covering Charlotte, Ferrisburgh, and Vergennes, Vermont. The newspaper's reportage was key in preserving two large acreage lakefront properties from commercial development. Following her picture book publication, she was a speaker in 44 Vermont classrooms and libraries. She has worked in a bookstore. She is the editor of Craig Burt's memoir, *We Lived in Stowe* (2003). An essay, "Early Morning Walks," (2015) is in *Open Doors: Stories from Wildlife Nation*. She is presently the editor of the *Chittenden County Historical Society Bulletin*, a quarterly, and was copy editor of the Vermont Farm Bureau quarterly, *Vermont Fences*. She has worked as a free-lance editor. Memberships include Society of Children's Book Writers and Illustrators, League of Vt. Writers, Poetry Society of Vermont, Vermont Historical Society, Chittenden County Historical Society, Charlotte Historical Society, and Vermont Farm Bureau. Her first published poem appeared in *Snowy Egret*, (Spring, 1997). Guided by her grandfather, an orchardist, and mother, a birder, her interest in nature, gardening, and hiking is life-long.

Douglas Scribner, graduate of Kansas City Art Institute, is a Stowe, Vermont, native. His cover painting is of his grandparents' farmhouse in Stowe Hollow. The sleigh is a fancy green Newport cutter.